On Talking Terms with Dogs: Calming Signals

Second Edition

Turid Rugaas

Dogwise Publishing
Wenatchee, Washington, U.S.A

On Talking Terms With Dogs: Calming Signals, 2nd edition.

Turid Rugaas

Dogwise Publishing
A Division of Direct Book Service, Inc.
403 South Mission Street, Wenatchee, WA 98801
www.dogwisepublishing.com

Originally published in Norway under the tilte
På Talefot Med Hunden, De Dempende Signalene

UK Editor Sheila Harper

Photographs by Turid Rugaas, Diana Robinson, Hilde Malm, Kirsten Berger, Gerd Groenwald, Gerd Köhler, Sheila Harper, Nicole Fröhlich, Sophie Hensley, Winkie Spiers and Cordelia Derrfuß

Cataloging-in-Publication Data is available upon request from the Library of Congress

ISBN: 978-1-929242-36-8

Printed in the USA

Contents

My everlasting gratitude and love to VESLA
who started it all, just by being herself

This book was written thanks to Terry Ryan, who nagged me into
doing it, helped me with art work for it, and had the first edition published. Thanks Terry!

Vesla's Story

The big Briard attacked violently and with a roar. He went for the little Elkhound at full speed. She stopped moving, stood quite still, and turned her head to one side. Just a few feet away from the Elkhound, the Briard stopped and looked bewildered as if he didn't know what to do. Then he started to look around for some replacement activity, sniffed a little at the ground, and turned to head back to base.

The place was my training field. The client was a Briard with dog-to-dog problems. The little Elkhound was my own Vesla, who was thirteen years of age.

Vesla always knows what to do and she always manages to calm down other dogs, whether they are aggressive, afraid, stressed or just being a nuisance. For eleven years no dog has been able to throw her off her mental balance. She is the image of a survivor, a conflict-solving dog with all the communication skills needed to survive.

Vesla wasn't always like that. She came to me as a stray dog. We meant to re-home her as she upset my own dogs with her aggressive and violent behavior. She fought, she quarrelled, she was stressed and she was impossible, and I didn't feel the right inclination to start to work with her. But nobody else wanted her, so with a sigh of resignation we kept her and started to try to incorporate her into our family of people and dogs.

It was a time of trials. I am sure she was the worst dog I have ever had in the house. Gradually, though, things got better. She stopped climbing the curtains. She could go for walks without trying to bite the others all the time. She could relax now and again.

And then one day I saw to my astonishment that she had actually started to communicate with the other dogs. Their work had started to get through to her! When I discovered that she actually was recovering her dog language, I tried my usual method for training. I praised every step in the right direction, and every time I caught a glimpse of a calming signal, I praised her. She became better and better at communicating. I realized to my surprise that it was possible to reinforce her own language by praising her, and then things happened very quickly. She was now helped by both my dogs and myself. In a very short time she was a miracle of dog language. One year after I got her, she had stopped all her aggressive behavior, and from then until today, twelve years later, she has not once been in trouble with any dog. They just cannot make her lose control.

The story of Vesla made me realize that it is possible to re-teach lost language to dogs. Since then I have made this teaching a life-style and my main job. And it has enriched my life: I now understand better and see better what dogs feel. I truly feel that I am on talking terms with the dogs. And that gives me a good feeling, just like the childhood dream about talking to animals.

Thank you Vesla, for all you taught me. It changed my life.

Author's note: This was written in 1996. Vesla died a few years later.

Foreword

The social dynamics of a wolf pack is often used as a model for dog-dog and dog-human interactions. I have seen dog people (and some wolf people as well) caught up in the idea of always maintaining high rank by aggressive means, believing their only choices are between forcibly dominating the animal or submitting to it. The problem with this approach is two-fold. Firstly, aggression may well escalate, and secondly, an either-or choice between forcible dominance or submission is not the only choice available to wolves, to dogs or to humans.

With what she calls "calming signals" based on canine expressive behavior, Turid Rugaas introduces dog trainers and owners to another option to try to improve relationships between humans and their dogs and between dogs and other dogs.   **Pat Goodman**

Foreword

The occasion was "Animals and Us," the Sixth International Conference on Human-Animal Interactions in Montreal. A quiet, polite seminar attendee, Turid Rugaas, sat a couple of rows ahead of me during the canine behavior sessions. Turid should never play poker. I couldn't help but notice her shoulders tensing up or relaxing depending on the speaker. The funny thing was, her body language was directly reflecting my own opinion of the various speakers' presentations.

Networking! That's what symposiums are all about! I wanted to meet this stranger from overseas whose response to behavior issues seemed to so closely mirror my own. Realizing that English was not her native tongue, and wondering if she would understand, it took me until the end of the day to gather the nerve to approach her. Since that meeting back in 1992, I have spent a lot of time with Turid. I've invited her to present at my behavior and training camps and seminars both in the United States and overseas. She has captivated her audiences wherever she goes. She was a big hit in Japan with her blue eyes and flaxen braids!

Turid's farm, Hagan Hundeskole, is located on a heavily forested mountain top overlooking scenic fiords of Norway. People from all over the country bring their dogs for her instruction in basic manners and rehabilitation of problem behaviors. I have been there to observe during her work with dogs and she has amazed me. The stories she tells in this book are true. I have come to realize that she is on the cutting edge of understanding canine behavior. The following quote from Turid gives the essence of her theory on calming-signals.

"Dogs, being flock animals, have a language for communication with each other. Canine language in general consists of a large variety of signals using body, face, ears, tail, sounds, movement, and expression. The dog's innate ability to signal is easily lost or reinforced through life's experience. If we study the signals dogs use with each other and use them ourselves, we increase our ability to communicate with our dogs. Most noteworthy of all canine signals are the calming signals, which are used to maintain a healthy social hierarchy and resolution of conflict within the flock. These are skills which, when carried over to our own interactions with dogs, can be highly beneficial to our relationship. Dogs have the ability to calm themselves in the face of a shock (fearful or stressful situation) and to calm each other as well. As an example let's consider the manner in which dogs meet each other. Dogs which are worried in a social situation can communicate concepts such as, 'I know you are the boss around here and I won't make trouble.' Furthermore, the boss dog is very apt to want the worried dog to realize that no trouble is intended. 'Don't worry, I'm in charge around here and I mean you no harm.' Dogs that do not signal properly can be the cause of problems."

On trips to Europe I make it a point to visit Turid's farm, Hagan Hundeskole, to observe her work. I have been on seminar tours with her in Europe, USA and Japan. Whether a training camp north of the Arctic Circle or national symposium in Geneva, each time she has left me favorably impressed with her ability to explain to her audience what is going on with dog at any given time.   **Terry Ryan**

1 Calming Signals: The Life Insurance Policy

In books about wolves you will find the body language of wolves described as "cut-off" signals, as the observers saw how they were cutting off aggression in other wolves. These signals have been described for years and are well known. The same people describing these signals seem to think that dogs do not have the same ability to cut off aggression in each other (*Behavior of Wolves, Dogs and Related Canids by* Michael Fox) – and how wrong they are! Dogs have the same ability and the same social skills to avoid conflicts as wolves have. Perhaps those observers did not see them, because the wolves are much more intense in their behavior due to their life situation. Dogs, that is domesticated dogs, are much more subtle in their skills and use much smaller letters, so to say. They are usually not in the same position of danger as wolves, and they do not have the same need to speak to each other in such big letters.

When I started to observe and use these signals, I called them calming signals. Cut-off is not the appropriate word, as they are used much more as prevention than really cutting off behavior. The signals are used at an early stage to prevent things from happening, avoiding threats from people and dogs, calming down nervousness, fear, noise and unpleasant things. The signals are used for calming themselves when they feel stressed or uneasy. They are used to make the others involved feel safer and understand the goodwill the signals indicate. They are also used to enable dogs to make friends with other dogs and people.

Dogs communicating their
peaceful intentions.

Conflict solving

Those dogs that are able to develop communication skills with other dogs, and that have not lost their signals because of us, understand each other and need never be in conflict with others. Wolves and dogs try to avoid conflicts. They are conflict-solving animals. It is usually we, the human species, who tend to create conflicts between our dogs and ourselves.

We will look more closely at these signals throughout this book, what they are and how they are used, in order to help you learn to understand your dog better and be a better "parent" for your dog. It will help you in training and handling, and I am certain that these new skills will enrich your life as they have mine.

How do they work?

Think about an average day with your dog. You get up in the morning, with the "Monday morning" feeling, and tell the dog off with a bit of annoyance in your voice. He turns his face sideways to you, and licks his nose in one quick movement. You wash, finish getting ready and go to the door. The dog is happy to know that he is going out and fawns around you. You command him "SIT"! The commanding tone makes your dog yawn before he sits down. You put on his leash, go out of the door and he pulls a little. You jerk him back, he then turns his back on you and puts his nose to the ground.

At the park you let him loose for a few minutes, and before long your wrist watch tells you that it is time to go back. You call your dog. Was your voice a little stressed? Your dog starts moving towards you slowly and in a curve. You think he does it to annoy you, and you yell at him. He sniffs the ground, curves even more, and looks away from you. He finally comes and you scold him or, even worse, you shake him. He turns his face from you, licking his nose or yawning.

This was only one morning's procedure. We could have gone through the whole day like this and told you step by step every time your dog tries to calm you down with his signals. These signals are there as soon as anything happens.

Dogs use the signals as soon as there is anything to calm down. If they are awake, they "talk," just like you and I.

Often the signals come in quick movements, so quick that we need to really look hard to be able to see them. With practice at observation and experience you learn to see these small flashes. Other dogs see them, even other animals, like cats. All it takes is a little practice and knowing what to look for.

Which dogs have these signals?

Wolves have them. Dogs have inherited them. All of the various breeds all over the world have them, no matter what size, color, or shape they are. They all have them. It is a truly universal language and a wonderful one because it means we can communicate with dogs wherever we meet them.

Just imagine being able to travel the world, and everywhere you go you can speak your native tongue, and everybody else understands because they all speak the same language. How marvellous that would be. I have been to the USA, Japan, England and many other countries, and I have seen it with my own eyes. Dogs speak the same language all over the world.

Some breeds or types of dog have certain signals that are better developed than others due to their different appearance. Black dogs, for instance, have a tendency to use licking more than other facial expres-

4

Many dogs lick their noses when a camera is pointed directly at them.

sions, although they understand dogs using other signals and they understand humans who use them.

Dogs and wolves have strong instincts for conflict solving, communication and cooperation.

Their repertoire also includes threatening signals, and when we are dealing with dogs we have a choice of how to behave: we can be calming, friendly or reassuring, or we can be threatening. Whatever we choose will have consequences for our relationship with the dog. When you are using threats to your dog, intentionally or unintentionally, the dog will use calming signals in order to try to calm you. For the conflict-solving dog, threats must be calmed down. I prefer to put it this way: Why on earth should we ever use threatening signals to dogs?

What signals are we talking about? We know at least 30 signals. Some signals are used for other things as well, in other situations. Some are so swift that we can hardly see them. It takes experience to see everything in every situation. But with experience and frequent observation, you will be able to catch a glimpse of them all, and you will always be able to tell how your dog is feeling. You will understand your dog much better. And isn't that what we would all like? To really understand how they feel?

"The greatness of a nation can be judged
by the way its animals are treated."

Mahatma Gandhi

2 Calming Signals: How to Identify and Use Them

Head turning

A signal can be a swift movement, with the dog either turning his head to the side and back, or holding his head to one side for some time. It can be just a tiny movement, or the whole head can be clearly and deliberately turned to the side for several seconds.

Your dog may use head turning to tell an approaching dog to calm down. Perhaps the other dog approached yours too quickly, or approached him directly head on instead of in a curve.

Have you ever noticed your dog turning his head when you try to take a photo of him? He's telling you that he feels uncomfortable with this.

Your dog may turn his head if you stoop over him. Although he may stand still, he might also turn his head which tells you that he is feeling uncomfortable in this situation.

🐾 You can use head turning yourself when a dog starts to get worried or frightened if you have approached him impolitely. If a scared dog starts to bark or growl at you, stop moving towards him, turn your head to one side and this will help him feel better.

How polite!
Each of these dogs uses a calming signals in order to avoid conflict.

For example, when two dogs meet, they usually both look away for a second, and then they greet each other happily. Often, when I go up to my dog Saga to take her picture, she finds the camera a bit scary. She looks away when I take the picture, but looks at me again when I remove the camera from my face.

A head turn diverts a direct gaze.

When one dog turns his head another will often answer by doing the same.

8

Softening the eyes

"Shortening the eye" by making the eyes look at another individual in a softer way, lowering the lids, and not staring in a threatening way, are signals. Your dog may use them when he looks at someone straight on but does not want to make himself seem threatening.

A non-confrontational approach: "shortening the eye" indicates peaceful intentions.

You can use a similar signal yourself if you wish to train the exercise "eye contact," making the contact softer and more friendly.

Good manners: averting the gaze.

Sitting down with your eyes at the same level as the dog might be threatening for some dogs. If you get the feeling that he actually feels threatened by it, you can stand up and look at him from above; this means that your eyes will become "shortened" and you will immediately seem to stare less. Many dogs find it difficult to have direct facial contact.

9

Turning away

Turning the side or back to someone is very calming. When dogs play together rather wildly, some of them will start turning their side or back to the others in between playing, to make things calm down a little.

Despite the dog on the right giving off calming signals, the dog on the left still feels threatened. He turns away to increase the distance and lessen the threat.

Your dog may use this signal when another dog growls or behaves threateningly towards him in some way, such as running up to him too quickly. He may also use it if you speak in a very cross voice or go up to him when he feels that you are angry. When young dogs pester older ones, the older often turns back to make them calm down. When you jerk at the leash your dog may turn away from you, maybe pulling even more.

 You can use this signal yourself when a dog shows signs of nervousness or aggression towards you. If he jumps up at you, turn away, and more often than not he will stop.

In the photo below, Julias has turned his head, then his side and finally his back to a very angry German Shepherd. By the time he had his back to her, the shepherd had actually become much calmer.

One dog will often turn away to avoid a threatening situation.

Raif turns away from the deerhound's impolite approach.

If your dog is overwhelming you by jumping up and bothering you, turn your back on the dog and he will quiet down. If you are approaching a strange dog and suddenly you see that the dog is becoming nervous, turn your back to him. In a few seconds the dog will come to you.

Gino, a Doberman Pinscher, was not happy with some young boys who had been pestering him a great deal. The owner taught the boys to turn their backs to Gino. Immediately Gino felt he could come up to them and they made friends.

If a dog jumps up, turn your back on him! This is a strong signal that dogs will respond to if used consistently.

Occasionally it seems as though one dog hasn't even noticed another. In fact it means that he is feeling rather vulnerable.

While jumping, this Dalmatian simultaneously turns away as he finds the woman's body posture threatening.

Below: The white dog sees another dog approaching directly. She stands still and turns her head indicating this is impolite behavior.

Above: Each dog does its best to calm the others in its choice of position or calming signal.

Left: Vesla feels uncomfortable when Gaby tries to attach a rope to her. Fortunately Turid takes her grand-daughter away, leaving Vesla in peace.

Licking the nose

You may notice a very quick movement of the tongue, flicking so quickly that sometimes it is hard to see this calming signal.

Your dog may use it when approaching another dog. When you bend over your dog or hold him tight, or when you bend down to grab him or talk to him in an angry voice, he may use this signal.

You may not be able to use it. It is one of the signals I often find awkward for people to use.

Rocky sees another dog in the distance coming his way. He stops, turns his head and licks several times.

This dog might be licking his nose to calm himself down as the camera is pointing directly at him, or he may be calming another person or dog out of the camera shot.

I bend over Vesla to clean her ears. She looks away and licks.

The veterinarian bends down to lift Ulla up on the table. She licks, showing that she is a little uncomfortable.

A direct approach and outstretched hands can be rather disconcerting.

Too many hands and too little space are making this youngster feel very uncomfortable.

Even a flick of the tongue can have a calming effect.

Freezing

Your dog may freeze: stopping, standing, sitting or lying still without moving a muscle when a much bigger dog comes up too close and starts sniffing him all over.

Lorry, a little Whippet, was greeted by a very big German Shepherd male dog who sniffed him all over. He stood as still as he could, freezing completely, until the dog moved off to look for other "prey." Finally he could move again.

A man who was training his dog for obedience became angry when his very young dog got up from a long down stay, curious to greet some other dogs he had seen approaching in the distance. The man was so angry that he started to yell, real aggression in his voice. The dog stopped and stood quite still. He didn't dare to move he was trying so hard to calm his owner down. The man ran up to him and really told him off for being so "stubborn."

A competitor got a new dog for competition work. Being very ambitious, with hopes of having a champion at an early age, he started training and correcting the puppy. Then one day when he called the dog, the dog stopped, sat down and didn't dare to move.

Saga does a wonderful job of calming simply by freezing to let the other dog know that she is not a threat.

Walking slowly, using slow movements

Movements that become slower, sometimes so slow that there is hardly any movement at all, have a very calming effect.

Your dog may use it when he spots another dog. The slow movements start at the sight of the other dog. They start when you call your dog, and you are a bit irritable or your voice is commanding. They start when there are a lot of things happening around the dog, and he tries to calm things down. When you jump and wave and scream a lot to make the dog run faster, it will often have the opposite effect. The dog gets slower in order to calm you down.

You can use it when a dog seems frightened of you, or when you do not want to scare a dog. When you approach a dog that you want to put on leash, the slower you move, the better chance you have of making him stand still.

For example

 Shiba, a Border Collie agility dog, became slower and slower on the agility course. The owner ran around, jumped up and down, waved her arms and yelled a lot to encourage the dog. In the end, Shiba hardly moved around the agility field because she was trying so hard to calm her owner.

 The owner is calling Candy to go home from the park. Some people and dogs stand between her and her owner, so Candy walks slowly past them before she continues to her owner.

 You say "down" in a harsh way. Your dog begins to lie down, but moves very slowly because he has to calm the anger in your voice.

18

This Dalmatian finds the training situation too much and releases tension by giving a bow.

Such communication can often be understood between species.

Play Bow

Bowing can be an invitation to play, particularly if the dog is jumping from side to side in a playful manner. If he stands still in a bow the possibility of it being a calming signal is high.

Your dog may use this when he wants to become friends with another dog who is a little sceptical of him or a bit nervous. He may use the bow when he meets another animal such as a horse or cow that he does not feel too sure about.

You can use a similar signal yourself by stretching your arms, rather like when you yawn, but stretching down towards the ground.

For example

 Vesla wanted Buster, a St. Bernard dog, to feel safe with her, so after having walked slowly towards him, turning her head from side to side, she stopped at some distance and went down in play position. She stood there for several seconds until Buster felt safe with her and then did the same to answer her signal.

 Little Pip the Chihuahua was scared of bigger dogs. When Saga came along, Pip went down in play position to make sure that Saga would be polite and nice to her. Saga answered her signal by moving slower, in a curve, and looking away.

 Prince, a Rottweiler, went down in play position when he met a Golden Retriever who was a little frightened. He stood there for several minutes, quite still, in order to make her feel better about him being there.

A bow is often done in play. However, here both dogs bow, hold their position and turn their heads to avoid conflict – a definite calming signal.

Sitting down

A dog that either turns its back to you while sitting down, or simply sits down when another dog is approaching, is signalling.

Your dog may use it when another dog is making him feel uncertain or when you yell to make him come.

You too can use this signal. Try sitting when your dog is stressed and cannot relax. Make your guests sit down if you have a dog that is not quite sure about strangers.

These dogs are calming down both the owner and each other.

Lying down is an even stronger signal.

For example

 Roscoe, a German Shepherd, turned his back to his owner and sat down whenever he was given a command. The command was given in a very strong voice, which evidently made the dog feel uncomfortable. I suggested that the owner talk to his dog in a normal, everyday voice, and the dog came to him.

 Once Saga was out with me when two fiercely barking strange dogs suddenly came running towards her. She is best at facial expressions, but it was getting dark so she had to be more clear about her feelings. She sat down as they came rushing towards her. They immediately slowed down, stopped barking, and came up to her, sniffing the ground. Saga is never in trouble with other dogs. She is very sure about how to handle any situation.

One dog gives a very clear signal by lying down as the other approaches.

Down

For a dog, lying down on his back, belly up, is submission. Lying down with his belly to the ground is an act of calming. It is a very strong one too, often used by high-ranking dogs like my Ulla, who had the role of parent in my pack.

Your dog may use it as a puppy when play gets too rough, or as an adult when young ones seem to be afraid of him. When dogs get tired during play and want the others to calm down they may use it.

You can use it when your dog is stressed and trying to get attention. Lie down on the sofa. If a dog seems to feel scared of you, not daring to come closer, lie down. In many cases he'll be there within a few seconds.

The vacuum cleaner makes this dog feel threatened. She lies down in order to indicate her discomfort at being in this situation.

For example

  A group of dogs were playing in my training field when some of them began to get excited. Ulla noticed that they were becoming overwhelmed, so she went to the middle of the field and lay down, sphinx-like. One by one the others noticed her clear signal. In a matter of minutes, they had calmed down and also lay down around her.

  A scared little dog didn't dare to approach Saga, who went into a down when she saw its fear. Gaining confidence due to this clear show of empathy, it only took a very short while for the scared dog to pluck up enough courage to make contact.

An adult dog was together with five puppies that were harassing him, obviously thinking he was a recycled toy! At first he was patient with them, but when they started to get too much he lay down. The puppies immediately responded, leaving him alone and playing with each other instead. When he got up, he was fair game, and they were at him once again.

Yawning

Yawning is probably the most intriguing of the calming signals and is one which people seem to enjoy using.

Your dog may yawn in many situations, such as when you go into the veterinarian's surgery, when there is a fight or quarrel in the family, when you hold your dog too tight, or when a child goes to hug him, for example.

You can use it when your dog feels uncertain, a little bit scared, stressed, worried, or when you want him to calm down a bit.

For example

 Ulla is easily excited when someone is running or playing. Playing with her might end with her biting at my trouser legs. When she starts to get excited, I stand still and yawn a little, and she relaxes.

Yawning is an intriguing signal.

My colleague Ståle came to my house when I was dealing with a client with a fearful dog. As Ståle came through the door he immediately noticed the dog's fear and responded to it by standing still and yawning several times. The dog was interested in him, then turned to me, and I yawned too. In a matter of minutes the dog was quite comfortable with us and made contact with him.

 Candy was restless and stressed one evening so her owner sat down, yawning frequently. Candy eventually stopped her restless wandering, laid down by the owner's feet, and relaxed.

 Little Sheila was loved very much by her owner. Once when I was there the owner picked Sheila up, put her on her lap and hugged her. Dogs feel uncomfortable in such a tight situation, so Sheila yawned and yawned.

Above: Tia uses the yawn frequently. Simply opening her mouth rather than giving a full yawn is enough for her to make her point.

Right: As yawning seems to be contagious, a dog will often answer a yawning dog with a similar signal.

Lucy and Sophie communicate by sniffing the ground.

Sniffing

Sniffing can be a swift movement down towards the ground and up again. Alternatively a dog may persistently stand with his nose down to the floor for some time until the problem situation is over. As dogs also sniff to explore smells, it is important to look at the whole situation to be sure what it is.

Your dog may sniff when another dog is approaching him, when someone is walking straight at him, or when a sudden situation occurs such as when another dog suddenly appears too close to him. When you walk along the road and someone is walking directly at you, maybe carrying a big hat or something, your dog may sniff. When you call your dog and your voice shows annoyance or is rather authoritative, or maybe when you are standing facing full on to the dog, he may be likely to sniff several times while coming.

Sniffing is one of those signals that are difficult for people to use. I find it hard to practice sniffing. But something similar can be used: you might try sitting down, pretending to scratch the grass or to examine something on the floor.

The Springer Spaniel turns sideways to Tia and sniffs giving a clear signal of a peaceful intention.

One signal is answered by another (sniffing and turning away).

A client with a very aggressive dog named King came to see me. She didn't dare to let him out of the car, as she was afraid he would kill any dog outside. I took Vesla with me, and let her go by herself outside the car. I told the owner to hold the leash and open the door of the car, letting the "aggressive" dog out. And out he came - a monster of little golden mix breed - all teeth, and foaming and barking his head off. He really looked fierce. Vesla was only yards away, and when King came out of the car door like a rocket, she just put her nose to the ground and kept it there. King was snarling and acting wildly. Vesla was sniffing, but suddenly she made up her mind, went straight up to him, nose to nose, and King deflated like a punctured balloon. Ten minutes later he was able to run happily with seven other dogs in the training field.

 When I walked with Ulla down in the village the other day, a man came towards us with a little dog barking on leash. Ulla went to the side of the road, put her nose to the ground, and stood there as they approached and passed.

 Candy was called by her owner in the park, and she ran happily after him. Suddenly another dog came up to her. Candy slowed down, sniffed the ground, the other dog went on his way, and she continued her happy running to join her master.

 Sara, a Doberman Pinscher, was left tied to a tree while her owner was doing something else. A man came towards her and she immediately turned side on to him and started to sniff the ground. She felt uncomfortable being approached by a stranger coming up to her while she was tied up, and tried to make him understand that. He did not understand, but I managed to help her by preventing him approaching her.

Sophie tries to help a visiting Bearded Collie feel at ease by lying down.

This heavy down signal soon elicits an answering sniff, and both make their point even more clearly by taking up a side-on stance.

With all the polite preliminaries out of the way, the two dogs can get closer and eventually make contact knowing that all will be well.

Slowing down
and curving
is an effective
introduction.

Curving

Curving or walking in a curve or at a little distance from another dog or a person is a signal. Mature dogs do not usually go straight toward each other. They might, if they use other clear signals, but it is impolite to do so and most of them try to avoid it.

Your dog will often curve when you meet someone coming towards you on the path. It is frequently used when something is approaching or is in the dog's way but where he still needs to go in that direction. When you walk with your dog by your side or in heel position and something comes towards him on that side, he might try to walk on the other side of you. If a dog looks fearful or angry, your dog will often use a wide curve around the dog in order to calm him down.

You can use this signal when approaching a fearful or aggressive dog or when you meet a dog that gives you a calming signal like sniffing, licking, head turning or something else. Sometimes you need to use a wide curve, or sometimes it is enough to change direction a tiny bit, just curving slightly past the dog. Watch the dog you are meeting, and curve as much as necessary to make the dog feel comfortable.

For example

 Candy met a Newfoundland puppy who was not very well acquainted with other dogs and who was afraid of her. Candy immediately walked around him in a wide curve, her nose to the ground.

 Max met another male dog while out walking and went in a curve past him.

 A German Wirehaired Pointer named Connie was with her owners at my home. They said that she was scared of people, and as I came walking across the room towards her she licked and looked away. I immediately changed direction and looked away from her passing her only feet away, but curving. She came up to me right away and made contact.

Curving to avert any conflict.

One dog curves and the other answers by turning away.

Splitting up

Physically putting one's body between dogs or people is a signal. When dogs, humans, or a dog and a human get too close, or if the situation is becoming tense, many dogs go in between to split up and to avoid any conflict arising.

Your dog may split up when you have a child on your lap and are making a lot of fuss of it, when you waltz or dance around with someone, or when you sit close together with your friend on the sofa. If two dogs become a little tense or if they are too close to each other, a third party, dog or human, may use this signal.

You can position yourself to split up dogs when they get tense, when your dog becomes uneasy or frightened in a situation, or when children are playing or doing things to dogs that make the dogs feel uneasy.

 In a puppy class some larger puppies started to be a little bit too rough with one of the smaller ones. Before I had the chance to do

One dog intervenes in a potentially threatening situation by going in between, turning his head and diffusing any contact.

anything about it, Saga went between them and took care of the small puppy. The others were not allowed close to the puppy.

 Two adult dogs were playing rather wildly. A puppy in the same room felt uneasy about the situation and hid under the owner's chair. Every time the other dogs came towards the puppy, he whined. Another adult dog, a Springer Spaniel named Dennis, came in through the door and went straight over to split them up to protect the little one. He stood beside the puppy, his side to the others, not allowing them close.

I was out walking Saga when we met a little Poodle. Suddenly a Samoyed approached, roaring, attacking the Poodle. Saga went right in between them and stopped the attack.

An unknown dog rushes up to Turid. Saga positions herself in between in order to calm any threat. The dog responds by turning and moving away.

Taku the Malamute wants to play, but the Springer Spaniel is concerned. The Springer lies down - a strong signal - and Taku answers by mirroring her. However, Border Collie Tia feels that this situation could escalate, so she carefully approaches ready to split up. She lifts her paw as an extra signal of good intent.

Tia waits for the right moment to intervene, ensuring that she poses no threat. She turns her head, careful to make no direct eye contact.

The two dogs are too close for Tia to safely split with her body, but she makes both dogs aware of her presence.

Wagging the tail

A wagging tail is not always a sign of happiness. In order to interpret it properly you need to look at the whole dog. If the dog is crawling towards you, whining or peeing, the wagging tail is a "white flag," trying to make you calm down.

Your dog will use it when you have lost your temper. He will be trying to make you calm down and be nice again.

You will find it difficult to use this signal, I have never been able to do so very effectively!

 Lobo's owner came home with a worried look on his face, as Lobo had chewed up something the previous day and his owner was worried that it had happened again. The worried brow made Lobo crawl towards him, wagging his tail wildly, in the hope that his owner might look less angry. Many owners interpret this as the dog feeling guilty but this is not the case: the dog is reacting to the body language of its owner.

 My daughter had yelled at her twin daughters. When she came into the yard where Saga was, Saga came up to her with a wildly wagging tail and smiling – everything she could possibly do to make her calm down.

 Cora, a German Shepherd, always greeted her owner by crawling, peeing and wagging tail. The owner had used a lot of shaking, yelling and pinching her ears. Cora was afraid of him every time she saw him, and her way of greeting him showed fear and also that she was desperately trying to calm him down.

A paw lift is another well-used signal.

There's more!

The signals discussed so far are the most commonly used signals in dogs. But dogs also calm others by "playing puppy" by making themselves small, trying to lick faces, blinking their eyes, smacking their lips, and lifting their paws.

 Right in front of me was a very aggressive Rottweiler who, by the sound of his deep growling, meant business and was intent on discouraging any interference in his privacy. The growling became deeper if I tried to move my head or something, so I had to stand still. I was certainly not going to back away, so all I could think of doing was blinking my eyes. After a while the growling ceased, and suddenly the Rottweiler's tail started to wag a little. From then on, it took me only a very short time to become his friend.

🐾 A scared little Basenji growled at a German Shepherd, who stood still lifting his paw up and down, licking his nose and blinking his eyes. All these signals were extremely effective in making the Basenji calm down.

These are all calming signals. Dogs also have other kinds of signals. Some are threatening, like staring, walking straight towards someone, standing over another dog, growling, barking, attacking and showing their teeth. Some only tell us about feelings of excitement or arousal inside the dog, such as raising their hackles and tails.

These signals are often misinterpreted, as they are easy to see and they are what people notice most. They tell us something about the dog's excitement in that situation, but don't be too preoccupied with them. Watch out for other signals indicating the dog is threatening or calming. They will tell you more.

Misty is a little worried about the camera. She turns her head away to calm herself, but needs to keep an eye on the camera just in case!

Develop your observation skills

Not only is it important to be able to see these signals in your own and other dogs, but it is also important for you to be able to help your dog. By knowing the signals yourself and understanding them well, you can identify the dog's signals when they happen.

If you have not been very aware of them before, you can teach yourself the skill of seeing them by training yourself.

At home

Spend some time at home sitting and just observing your dog. In a quiet home atmosphere you will not get many signals, but do so anyway as a start. Then, once someone moves or walks around the house, or when visitors arrive, something will happen where your dog will give off signals and then you can observe what he is doing.

With other dogs

Now, make use of every situation where your dog is meeting other dogs. Go to the park perhaps, or somewhere where dogs are off leash and then you can concentrate on what your dog is doing. Every time your dog meets another dog, look at him the second he sees the other dog at a distance, and notice which signals he is using.

As the camera points towards the dogs, both turn their heads to calm the situation.

This Terveuren could be licking because of the camera, or he may be trying to calm down the youngster.

One at a time

A third way of observing is to decide on one signal you would like to be able to identify. Perhaps you have already noticed some signals your dog is using. Maybe you recall that you have seen him licking or yawning now and again. Then decide that for the next weeks you will try to watch out for licking every time you see a dog. Keep an eye on the dog just being there, to see if the licking occurs. It will take some concentration from your side in the beginning, but it will become almost automatic with practice.

When you feel sure that you see licking whenever it happens and can understand how the dog is using it, then start observing one or two more signals. Since head turning occurs frequently, perhaps you could observe that, and maybe curving or sniffing.

In a short time you should find yourself reading all dogs you see. It becomes a kind of an interesting hobby and you get more and more hooked on to the more you do it.

Welcome to the world of dog language!

3 Some Case Histories

Pippi

Pippi, a five-year-old German Shorthaired Pointer, was brought to see me because, her owner said, she was dangerously aggressive toward other dogs. On approaching my house, Pippi's owner stopped down the road, not daring to bring her dog any closer. Pippi looked calm and nice, greeted me politely, and seemed to be a dog you could live with. Her owner looked pale and stressed, and said that she was scared about what was going to happen.

I told her briefly what I was about to do, and she turned even paler, looking as if she was likely to faint. I told her to stand still, not to say anything, not to do anything, and that she could give me the leash if she wanted to. No, she wanted to hold Pippi herself. And then I called for my little Elkhound, Vesla, who had been waiting around the corner of the house, and she came. The second Pippi saw Vesla she was ready to start attacking and barking.

At a glance Vesla had taken the whole situation into consideration. She stopped and stood still for a second with her nose to the ground. This made Pippi stand still instead of leaping. Then slowly Vesla started to move in curves towards Pippi, nose to the ground, her side always to Pippi. Vesla's language was so clear that Pippi stood fascinated looking at her instead of attacking. Getting closer, Vesla became even slower and the last few yards took several minutes to cross. Pippi then put her nose to the ground too, and there they stood, sniffing the same spot, without looking at each other.

Pippi's owner came back several months later. She arrived while I was in the middle of a lesson, so I had a group of puppies around me. Pippi was let out of the car, went quietly over to one of the puppies and licked him. She had changed her attitude to other dogs completely.

This is a typical Vesla story. For twelve years she changed the lives of dogs who could no longer communicate with others.

A crouch and lip lick are both aiding commu- nication.

Buster

Buster, a big St. Bernard dog, was afraid of other dogs. Whenever he saw one, he hid behind his owner and had a really worried look on his face.

Buster and his owner stood waiting for us on the path down to my farm when I let Vesla out. Being fond of every dog she met, she ran up the path to meet Buster as soon as she spotted him. But then she saw something in the other dog's face, eyes or attitude that made her change her happy demeanor. She stopped running cheerfully towards him with a wagging tail. Instead, she started to move slowly, her head turned slowly and very distinctly from side to side as she walked, using no direct eye contact, no speed. The big dog stood there, evidently understanding the message she gave him. Some twenty feet away from him she stopped, going down and stretching out her front legs in what we call a play position, only this time it was not to invite him to play. She just stood there until she saw something in his eyes that invited her to go even closer. He did not make any attempt to retreat, but simply watched her. Then suddenly he too went down stretching out his front legs, and within seconds they had made direct contact.

Vesla saw his worries, understood what to do, and did her job, making him feel less worried. They communicated, they understood each other, and therefore could solve the problem – helping Buster to conquer his fears.

 Dogs are experts at this. Conflict solving is a part of their heritage from their ancestors the wolves, and they read each other like we read books. It is a part of their survival instincts and pack behavior. We will never be as good at it as the dogs are, but we can understand more about what they are telling us. We can observe, understand, and let the dog know we understand. We can give signals back to reassure them we understand. We can communicate better during training and daily life together with our dog.

🐾 We can learn the language of dogs in order to communicate better, have a better relationship with our dogs, and to do a better job in teaching them and bringing them up. We can avoid conflicts and also reduce the risks of having scared, insecure, aggressive and stressed dogs. We also reduce the risk of getting into dangerous situations ourselves, being injured and bitten as a result of the dog's self defense.

Expert conflict solving! Riley and Dennis position themselves carefully to avoid conflict.

The Hunting Dog

The slim hunting dog stood shaking in the middle of the room shivering, panting, looking desperate. She was a pitiful sight; so thin that her ribs stood way out. Within a few seconds the train near the house had passed, and then she started to behave more normally, coming up to greet me, being friendly, as these dogs usually are.

She lived beside the railway, and she was scared to death of the sound of trains when she was inside the house. She had become restless, had lost fifteen pounds in a short time, and had developed an abnormal heartbeat.

I was not at all sure what to do. Move to another house? Use drugs? I decided to try something when the next train came.

I told the owners what to do, and when the faint sound of the train appeared, I sat yawning and stretching my "front legs," avoiding eye contact with the dog, but looking out of the corner of my eye to see her reaction. The owners were to look another way, talk normally to each other and drink their coffee. She shivered and panted, but looked at me when I was yawning. She looked at her owners and back again. The panting was not as heavy this time. Could this be possible?

While the next train was passing, everybody sat yawning and did not look at the dog. There was a definitely a positive reaction in her.

I gave the owners some homework to do, and I returned one month later. They did not call me during that time, so I knew that the situation had not worsened. I came into the house with the dog greeting me like an old friend. I sat down, and she jumped up onto the sofa beside me (something that was allowed!) and curled herself up comfortably, falling asleep.

She had clearly put on weight and her ribs were not sticking out anymore. As we sat there, the sound of the approaching train began, coming closer and closer. The dog looked up at me with one eye, saw that I was still yawning, seemed to say, "Yes, that's what I thought", and promptly fell asleep again.

I was speechless and so happy. It was possible to reach through to a scared dog by using her own language, calming her fear. Once she had become calmer still her owners would be able to use some fun activities when they knew a train was coming, and that would also help .

This dog was one of my very first clients on whom I used calming signals, so I will never forget her.

I met her years later and she still recognised me. She lived to be an old and healthy dog, hunting rabbits in the forests. And now, I believe, if there are forests in heaven, she is still happily hunting there.

Saga

Saga was helping me shovel snow down the farm road, when some people suddenly showed up with two dogs off leash.

The dogs saw Saga and with a roar they both started running towards her, sounding and looking really fierce. I immediately started to move towards Saga in order to get between them, but it became clear that I could stop and simply let things happen. Saga had already done her job. When they came rushing towards her, she turned her back on them and sat down.

Saga's action immediately took the energy out of the strange dogs. They slowed down, stopped barking and started to sniff the ground. They actually never went all the way up to Saga. They stopped at a distance and stood still, quietly sniffing the ground.

Saga did not bother to make contact with them. Because they were behaving so badly to her, it took away any interest of friendship.

The two dogs turned and ran after their owner.

Saga turns her back on a Setter to encourage a calmer approach.

The Tibetan Mastiff

The Tibetan Mastiff was brought to me by his new owner. In a normal voice the man asked the dog to sit, but at the same time he bent over him. The dog immediately shut down as his contact with reality became distorted, retreating from this world to an inner world where no harm could reach him.

These gentle giants with the deep and growling voices are so misunderstood, and someone had done something to make this dog afraid of being alive, unable to cope with the real world.

The dog sat there, completely lost, and the owner tried to pull at him. I asked him to let it be. I went over and sat down beside the dog, looking in the same direction as he was, gently stroking his chest with very slow movements, all the while yawning and breathing deeply.

I sat there for fifteen to twenty minutes and gradually the dog started to come back to reality. He seemed bewildered, almost looking through me. He began to yawn, still sitting there hardly moving, not a threatening thing in sight. It took him some time to be conscious, but then he licked me and looked at me, apparently feeling safe.

He loved me to bits after that. I think I could have done anything with him. He had total trust in me and would hardly ever leave my side while he was visiting me with his owner.

It takes so little to be friendly to a dog, and the result can be so overwhelmingly huge. You have always the choice of being threatening or calming. To me the choice is easy.

Is your dog being "stubborn" or "distracted" or just walking away sniffing as a result of your actions? It might be that the dog is feeling a little insecure, not coping or perhaps unsure of how to deal with the situation. Be patient and give him time. Or you can help him by taking him out of this situation or by being less demanding and he will soon feel more comfortable.

The dog on the far left is finding the whole situation too demanding. She moves away and turns her back.

Chief Dan George

If you talk to the animals,

They will talk to you,

And you will know each
other.

If you do not talk to them,

You will not know them,

And what you do not know,

You will fear.

What one fears,

One destroys.

4 The Stressed Dog

Stress hormones are necessary for us. We need some quantity of them to be able to work, to have enough energy to do things we have to or want to do. Sometimes we are in situations that make us scared, upset, very excited or angry. As a result we get more hormones moving around our bodies. Then the adrenalin starts pumping.

How it works

You are out driving, and suddenly you have a close accident. You manage to get to safety, but within a few minutes your heartbeat begins to race and you get sweaty palms. You become upset or angry, you feel shaky or thirsty, or you want to go to the toilet. All kinds of reactions will tell you that your adrenalin level is high.

We humans become stressed in the face of accidents, anger, violence, and other things that provoke excitement; but first and foremost we get stressed in situations where we do not feel we can cope. Something is threatening us, and we are not sure about our ability to manage.

Dogs get stressed for the same reasons. They become stressed in situations of threat, of pain or of discomfort. They become stressed when we are angry or punish them. Excitement stresses them, such as when male dogs scent bitches in season. Lots of full speed action might stress a dog. But primarily a dog gets stressed for the same reason as humans: when they feel unable to cope.

When dogs start to get stressed, they can show it in many ways. When they are stressed by the environment, you will usually see that they start using calming signals to try to ease the stress. So knowing the calming signals will also help us to see when a dog starts to feel stressed.

Scientific research has given us more information about stress. In Scandinavia studies have been done of parachutists, pilots, divers and others who frequently deal with situations of danger.

A dog with a constantly high stress level will be much more likely to get stomach problems, allergies and heart trouble. They will be faster and more violent in their defense. They will probably have an activated defense mechanism at a much earlier point than others.

I work a lot with dogs who attack, lunge at people or dogs, and behave aggressively in many situations. Their defense mechanism is activated much earlier: they will react faster and more fiercely towards a threat than most dogs.

It all fits in.

An excited German Shepherd uses a play bow to communicate his intentions.

The adult Alessi (on the left in the photos below), is a little uncertain of some dogs, and immediately the nine month old puppy on the right understands.

Maya, the puppy, already has a highly developed series of signals to communicate her peaceful intentions.

Interactions such as this one are an everyday occurance in the lives of dogs. But what do their signals mean and how can we interpret them?

At first Maya gives heavy calming signals: sitting and turning right away.

As both dogs become more comfortable Maya relaxes her position, remains sitting, keeps her head turned away and blinks.

To end the encounter she checks on Alessi and moves away.

Example One

Many dogs have a high stress level because of demands resulting from a young age, anger and aggression from the owner's side, or being constantly commanded to obey, with the owner often using a harsh voice. A dog such as this is stressed by these things every day. As a result, stress levels remain high, and consequently the dog never calms down. This dog will also have a very high degree of self-defense. He is the one to behave aggressively towards other male dogs or people.

This dog's aggressive behavior might be learned. There is a slight possibility that some of it may be genetic. However, there is a high probability that this is a simple reaction to a life that makes him stressed. His owner's anger and demands make him unable to cope with daily life. He gets stressed. Together with the stress, it is also extremely likely that there will be a much higher level of self-defense, which is all too often the problem the owner comes to me with.

Very often these dogs suffer from illnesses such as stomach problems or allergies or show problem behaviors like fear, aggression or barking.

Example Two

Dogs learn by association. When, every time he sees another dog, he is being jerked on lead to make him heel or stop barking at the other dog, he will associate other dogs with a painful neck or back. Each time he sees another dog he will become stressed more and more quickly, and, in addition his defense mechanisms, will become much more rapidly activated by the heightened stress. A dog under this kind of pressure is also likely to behave aggressively toward other dogs, often to both males and females.

🐾 **This leads up to my conclusion:** There is **no,** absolutely **no**, reason or excuse to punish, be violent, threatening, or forceful towards a dog or to demand too much of him.

All of these things will make a dog stressed. In time, the stress will make him ill. He will become reactive more quickly, showing aggression to dogs or people, because he has a higher defense mechanism. It may end by him biting someone.

We always have a choice of how to behave. Then we can understand our dogs' calming signals and tell them that we understand. Or, we can overlook the signals and make the dog feel he cannot cope, consequently making him stressed.

If we behave in a threatening manner or in a way that makes the dog become unsure, scared, and defensive, there will be consequences. Sometimes this defense will be seen as fear. Some dogs have more flight defense, and they will try to escape, look afraid, be nervous or look like it. The fight defense will look like aggression.

When going through some of the enormous amount of material I have collected about scared and aggressive dogs, I can clearly see how this fits in.

Aggression, or defense, is a symptom. Very often a high stress level, because of environment, is the cause.

We must try to treat the underlying reasons for the behavior, not merely look at the symptoms. That will not get us very far.

Look at your dog's stress level. Find the reasons why your dog is stressed. By looking critically at yourself and your surroundings, you can often find out a lot all by yourself. Sometimes it can be helpful to ask someone to help you see the situation from the outside. We often become blind to what we do.

What makes the dog stressed?

- direct threats (by us or other dogs) such as violence, anger, aggression in his environment
- jerking at the lead, pushing him down, pulling him along
- too many demands in training and daily life

- too much exercise for young dogs
- too little exercise and activity
- hunger, thirst
- not having access to his toilet area when he needs it
- temperature - too hot or too cold
- pain and illness
- too much noise
- being alone
- sudden scary situations
- too much overexcited playing with balls or other dogs
- never being able to relax, always being disturbed

- sudden changes

Scratching is often the dog's way of showing stress.

How can we identify stress?

- inability to calm down, restless
- overreaction to things happening (for instance the doorbell ringing or a dog approaching)
- use of calming signals
- scratching
- biting himself
- biting and chewing furniture and shoes and other things
- barking, howling, whining
- diarrhea
- smell – both body or mouth giving off a bad odor
- tense muscles
- sudden "attack" of dandruff, for instance
- shaking
- change of eye color
- licking himself
- chasing his tail
- fur that seems to be hard, breakable, standing on end
- generally looking unhealthy
- panting
- losing concentration – inability to concentrate for more than a very short time
- shivering
- loss of appetite
- going to the toilet more often than normal
- allergies - many allergies are really stress, scratching
- fixation on certain things - glimpses of light, flies, crackling of firewood
- looking nervous
- behaving aggressively
- using displacement behavior when you ask him to do something

Several signs indicate that this dog is not entirely comfortable, including turning the head, looking away, open mouth and light panting.

What can we do about stress in our dogs?

It is not my intention to discuss all the things we can do to release stress in dogs - that would take another book by itself. However, here are a few basic ideas:

 Change environment and routines wherever possible.

 Stop using harsh methods, violence and painful things in training and handling, there is no excuse for it, and the dog's reaction to it shows us how valueless it is.

 We can teach ourselves to see, identify and use calming signals.

 Avoid putting the dog in a situation where he experiences hunger, thirst, heat, or extreme cold.

 Ensure that he has the opportunity to go to the toilet as often as he needs to. Try to find your dog's correct level of exercise and activity: too much or too little is not good for him.

 Let the dog be a part of his pack as much as possible: in other words, allow your dog to be with you or someone in the family, and teach him only very gradually to accept being alone.

🐾 Closeness, touching, massage, lying close together without keeping your dog there by force: all of these provide stress release for puppies as well as adult dogs.

Break the cycle

Fear tends to make dogs more stressed. The stress activates defense, which makes the dog more fearful. Where do we start to break up this bad circle?

One of the best ways to reduce stress is to be able to communicate with dogs. When you can make yourself understood by dogs, it is a wonderful feeling - for people and dogs alike. Calming signals are the key and seeing through that opened door has been like looking into a childhood dream of talking to the animals.

These dogs in a sit-stay in an obedience situation are finding it stressful. Each looks away from the other dogs, doing his best to calm himself and the others despite knowing that he is expected to stay in this position.

You can also begin to help your dog by stopping all force, punishment, aggression and anger towards him. Stop being threatening and start using calming signals. Your dog will understand and answer you back, and he will feel a lot better if you are friendly.

Feeling better is a good start to a new life!

Both dogs turn their heads away from the child staring directly at them.

5 Using Signals in Practical Handling and Training

When you are training the dog to lie down or sit, do not bend over him. Bend your knees or stand upright. You might turn your side to the dog especially if he doesn't like the exercise. Bending over will make the dog move slower, or he may try to avoid doing it completely.

Do not stoop towards the dog coming to you. If you do, in most cases he won't come all the way up to you at all, but will run past you, looking away from you. Stand upright, maybe with your side to the dog and then it is much more likely that he will come right up to you.

Do not jerk or use a tight leash when commanding your dog to heel. It hurts, it is painful to the neck, and makes the dog try to turn away from you, sniffing the ground or giving off other calming signals. Keep the leash loose – make a smacking sound with your tongue when you want the dog's attention, turn away from him in a right hand circle and the dog will follow if he is not dragged along or jerked at. A smacking sound, some praise and a turn to the right - that is all it takes, and it is much more pleasant than getting a sore neck.

Do not hold a dog tight. He can learn to accept it, but work on this has to be done very gradually.

It is much better to move your body in a way the dog can easily accept. For example, turn your side to the dog. If you have to crouch down low, don't bend over, but bend your knees instead, turning away from the dog. If you want to stroke the dog, start touching him down low, stroking his chest or under his chin. Do not hold him tight. Never try to hug a dog you do not know very well.

There are always some ways that will be less threatening than others. A dog should not feel threatened while doing things for you. Remember, you always have a choice! The following illustrations show techniques you can use to calm your dog.

Sitting close and putting your arm over the dog's back will often make him feel uncomfortable as this dog shows by yawning.

If you have a dog that is a little worried by another dog, walking parallel with human barriers in between will make him feel more comfortable.

Over time the distance between dogs can be narrowed.

Eventually the human barriers can drop out one at a time until the dogs are walking parallel with confidence.

Allow your dog a long enough leash so that he can show another dog how he feels by using calming signals. Don't pull on the leash, keep it slack and he will cope much better with the situation.

Curving away from another dog will also help both feel more comfortable as this is their natural language.

If one dog is approaching another head on, someone "splitting up" by going in between them will help the dogs.

6 What Happens When a Dog Loses its Language?

This is a question I often get. Dogs can't lose their language completely because the language is a part of their genetic heritage, and they are born with it. However, they can suppress their signals if they get punished for using them, or have ever been attacked when they used them.

I have had experiences training dogs that seem to have no language at all. A young dog or a very stressed dog will often not use calming signals in a stressful situation. The reason for this is that often, when stress arises, the brain doesn't function logically. It is possible to help a dog like this by making the situation easier to cope with, by creating enough distance between the dog and what it percieves as threatening, letting the dog face fewer threats, or allowing the dog to have the time to watch what is going on. Then the signals will return.

By simply allowing the dog to have more distance, he will be able to cope better and will feel more relaxed. Even better is to walk parallel to what he is worried about: using a barrier can also be a good idea, a barrier made of people if he is worried about dogs, or dogs if he is worried about people, for example.

Another thing to do is teach ourselves and our dogs to walk on a loose leash so that they get no pull or jerk on the leash, as mentioned in the previous chapter. The slightest discomfort when looking at another dog will ensure he has a negative association with that dog.

As we have seen, dogs learn by direct association, and so we must always be careful what signals we give to the dog when he looks at another dog, a person or a child. If we want him to form positive associations, to have positive feelings about anything, we must only give positive signals. In that way we can change a dog's association with absolutely anything and anybody.

If situations get a little tight or people, dogs or objects come too close, always let your dog have an "emergency exit" and let him use it if he feels like it.

The change of association can be a miraculously quick way of helping a dog to feel better about a situation.

7 When Do Puppies Start Using Calming Signals?

Some years ago I persuaded an English colleague to observe puppies. She did a lot of rescue work and always had an amazing number of dogs in her house, many of them pregnant and thrown out by someone. They had their puppies in her house, so she had a lot of opportunities to observe newborn litters.

This colleague observed litters during a two year period from the day they were born until they left 9-10 weeks later, and I received the results of her observations.

It was obvious that newborn puppies could not use many calming signals, as they have very little control of their bodies at that time, and often the only signal they could give was yawning. They yawned particularly when they were picked up and handled, and they did that from the very first day. One puppy was no more than seven hours old when he gave his first calming signals.

All of the puppies yawned 100 percent of the times they were picked up, from day one. Since then we have observed litters born in the safety of their own home with no stress of being moved or thrown out, and in these cases the calming signals would come days later.

The signals increase as the puppy grows older and have more control of their bodies, and when puppies turn up in my puppy classes they seem to master them all, or understand them all.

In order for puppies to become better at communicating and have the best opportunity of coping with other dogs, it is so important that they have the possibility of being together with other dogs all the way: all kinds of breeds, sizes, colors and appearance. It is the best education your dog can get, and it will save you so many problems later. Social and environmental training are definitely the two most important things in a puppy's education.

This puppy wants to make contact but is aware of the older dog's heavy calming signal.

The puppy responds by sitting.

She then continues by sniffing but still the older dog remains in a down.

The puppy finally gets the message that contact is not an option, and so she politely turns away, keeping an eye on the other dog.

Even as she moves further away she continues to indicate her peaceful intentions by dipping her head as if sniffing.

With the increased distance the puppy gets a response as the other dog begins to sniff.

Using a combination of slow movements, standing still and curving, the two dogs approach.

Contact at last! Thanks to skilful communication it's another successful interaction.

8 Leadership and Parenthood

For many years it has been a myth that you have to take a leadership position to prevent a puppy from trying to take over and to be the boss. Many sad dog destinies and many problems have come out of that myth, and it is not the way it works.

Stop using the word leadership, and use instead the word parenthood, as this is exactly what it should be.

A wolf pack is created by a pair of wolves who have cubs. The cubs grow up with the most patient and loving parents anyone can wish for, and in return they will love and have a natural respect for their parents lasting their whole lives. They are fed first, before the adults even think about eating, and they grow up in a world of love, safety and care.

When they get old enough, some of them will leave to make their own little family. Others stay with their parents, helping to bring up the new cubs, and hunt together with them. They never try to "take over" or anything like that as the natural respect lasts a lifetime.

When the puppy comes to new owners who start disciplining the puppy, punishing it or telling it off, it scares the puppy who is totally unprepared for this kind of treatment. The puppy's world becomes scary, frightening, and it might start to growl out of fear because of all this aggression he was not prepared for. Then he is punished for growling out of fear, and so problems start to occur, and the puppy's life becomes a misery.

The little puppy came to you totally trusting, and sees you as its new mother. He expects you to be as caring and loving as his own mother has been, and expects to be treated in the way he is used to.

Forget about being a leader of your puppy. Start being a parent.

The little puppy should learn a few rules and things, but not all at once, and absolutely not in a scary way. Look at how good dog mothers do it. They are so skilled at it and we have so much to learn from them. We often forget to teach them what we would like them to do and instead punish them for doing the wrong thing. However, they are not even capable of understanding the difference between right and wrong. In the life of dogs there is no "right" or "wrong" in the moral sense of the word. Dogs have to learn what we think is good or bad.

Until they are about 4 - 4½ months of age, puppies have a "puppy license" and can practically do whatever they like without the adult being telling them off. Why do we people so easily turn to violence? Think about how scary it must be for a little puppy to be threatened and physically abused by someone many, many times its size.

The dog will gradually suppress his own language and will learn nothing but the language of anger and aggression. Nobody cares about his feelings. As a result a dog may become introverted and may not dare to do anything, or he might become nervous and frightened, stressed and aggressive. Dogs treated in this may give up being dogs. They become problem dogs, because they have problems.

A safe, secure, patient and friendly puppy-hood and adolescence will give the dog the very best basis for growing up to be a harmonious, well-functioning adult dog.

Remember that wolves bringing up wolf cubs get perfect wolves out of them, and dogs bringing up puppies get perfect dogs out of them. When we humans bring up puppies, we get problems.

It is about time we looked at leadership as a myth we do not need. We need to be parents, good parents, the way dogs are good parents.

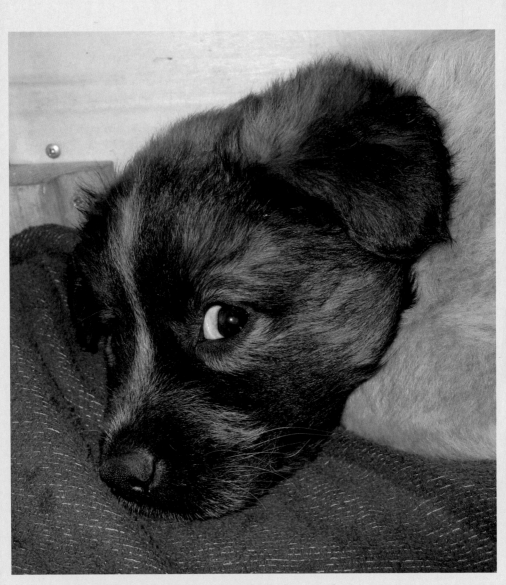

All puppies need security and stability. We need to protect our puppies, to allow them choices and to teach them with kindness. Only then will we really gain their trust, allowing a relationship to develop based on mutual respect.

9 Your Choice

When you have learned to read your dog and understand what the dog is telling you, you will have a better relationship with your dog.

Until now much of the relationship has consisted of a one-way communication: I, the owner, tell you what to do and you do what I say. This has nothing to do with a relationship.

Remember that every time you are close to a dog, you have a choice how to behave. You can act in a threatening or a friendly way. There is no, absolutely NO, excuse for scaring a dog. Dogs are survivors. They defend themselves when they feel threatened. Some will try to get away, others may answer back, and whatever solution the dog decides upon, it is you who made it happen.

By telling your dog you are friendly, it does not need to feel insecure in your presence. It can change the whole relationship to your dog.

You always have a choice. Whatever the situation, dog or incident you have always this choice of what to do. You can make tiny changes like looking away instead of staring, walking slowly instead of marching or running, turning away or standing still. Or you can accept that your dog is giving you a calming signal to tell you that he is tired, or cannot concentrate any more, or that he needs a break, for example.

If you want your dog to respect you, you must also respect your dog. A good relationship is based on two-way communication, and living together in a well-balanced togetherness. Leadership does not solve anything; it only creates problems, in our lives as well as in the dogs' lives.

It is your choice.

Epilogue

As a five year old I had a great wish for growing up doing "something for dogs."

I did not know what, since I didn't know what there was to do. As years went by the wish only became stronger, and I started on the road that led me up to my own flourishing dog training school and my desire was fulfilled.

I feel I reached my goal and even went far beyond it. I hoped for helping dogs in my neighborhood - I have already been to several parts of the world. I train close to 1,000 dogs every year, many of them being helped to a better life. I even received a big money prize for my work with dogs. I believe I must be the only dog trainer that has achieved that.

I also know for certain that the ultimate goal can never be reached. There will always be new dogs needing help, it is a never-ending story. But I know now where my road is winding, and I am more occupied by the road itself than of what is hiding round the next corner.

I feel privileged to be able to do what I have always wanted to do. I will go on doing it until the end of my days, using all my skills, my energy, and knowledge to help as many dogs as I can - doing something for dogs, because they have done so much for me.

About the Author

Turid Rugaas has spent most of her life with animals. A former racehorse trainer, Turid has always known instinctively that kind methods are the most effective, and has worked in this manner with any animal coming into her care.

She is founder of Hagen Hundeskole in Norway, training dogs and their owners, and spends most of her time travelling around the world to deliver her message.

Best known for her work on calming signals, studied at the end of the 1980's along with a colleague, Ståle Ødegaard, Turid produced her first book in 1996, with a video /DVD that followed shortly afterwards.

Turid is a founding member and President of the Pet Dog Trainers of Europe, an organization devoted to teaching through kindness and respect.

Turid and Star

Bibliography

Clothier, Suzanne	*Bones Would Rain From the Sky* Time Warner, 2002.
Coppinger, Ray and Lorna	*Dogs - A New Understanding of Canine Origin, Behavior and Evolution* University of Chicago Press, 2001.
Eaton, Barry	*Dominance, Fact or Fiction* 2002.
Engel, Cindy	*Wild Health* Pheonix, 2002.
Fox, Michael	*Behavior of Wolves, Dogs and Related Canids.* Florida: Krieger, 1987.
Lorenz, Konrad	*Man Meets Dog.* London: Methuen, 1954.
Lorenz, Konrad	*On Aggression.* New York: Harcourt, Brace and World, 1966.
Mech, L. David	*The Wolf: The Ecology and Behavior of an Endangered Species.* Minnesota: University of Minnesota Press, 1981.
Rugaas, Turid	*My Dog Pulls. What Do I Do?* Dogwise Publishing, 2005

Many of these books and others by these authors are also available from the extensive mail order section of dog-related books, videos, and training equipment at:

www.dogwise.com/1-800-776-2665

By the same author

Calming Signals: What Your Dog Tells You DVD

by Turid Rugaas

The companion to Turid's best selling book: On Talking Terms With Dogs is now available on DVD. Turid presents us with a unique opportunity to see footage of dogs using calming signals, increasing our own ability to study and observe the signals. Turid, who is the foremost authority in the world on dog language, gives explanations and shows us how we can use calming signals in our own interactions with dogs. Become an addictive dog-watcher with this fascinating, compulsive viewing.

Now you too can truly be "on talking terms with dogs"!

Viewing time: approximately 45 minutes.

Dogwise Publishing, 2005

What Do I Do When My Dog Pulls?

by Turid Rugaas

Norwegian dog trainer Turid Rugaas, best known for her ground-breaking work on calming signals, describes her kind and effective method for encouraging dogs to walk without pulling.

Quick and easy to learn, the method can be applied to any dog no matter what size, breed or age. Dogs that are easily distracted, or that encounter situations where they may lunge, bark or give aggressive displays can be helped to walk calmly and quietly on a slack leash. City, town or country walking can all become more relaxed, reducing stress for dog and owner.

Turid's method is explained in simple steps with informative photographs which aid understanding, and the book includes tips on equipment to use, reasons for pulling and trouble shooting, along with case studies.

Dogwise Publishing, 2005

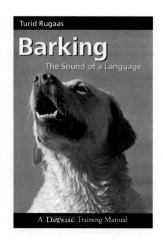

Barking: The Sound of a Language
by Turid Rugaas

Barking is natural and almost all dogs bark. It is one of the many ways dogs communicate with each other as well as with humans. In this book, author Turid Rugaas, well known for her work on identifying and utilizing canine "calming signals" to interpreting behavior, turns her attention to understanding and managing barking.

Think of barking as your dog's language. By learning to identify what your dog is expressing when he barks, you can take steps to minimize their negative effects.

Dogwise Publishing, 2008

BEHAVIOR & TRAINING

ABC's of Behavior Shaping; Fundamentals of Training; Proactive Behavior Mgmt, DVD. Ted Turner

Aggression In Dogs: Practical Mgmt, Prevention & Behaviour Modification. Brenda Aloff

Am I Safe? DVD. Sarah Kalnajs

Barking: The Sound of a Language. Turid Rugaas

Behavior Problems in Dogs, 3rd ed. William Campbell

Brenda Aloff's Fundamentals: Foundation Training for Every Dog, DVD. Brenda Aloff

Bringing Light to Shadow. A Dog Trainer's Diary. Pam Dennison

Canine Body Language. A Photographic Guide to the Native Language of Dogs. Brenda Aloff

Clicked Retriever. Lana Mitchell

Dog Behavior Problems. The Counselor's Handbook. William Campbell

Dog Detectives. Train Your Dog to Find Lost Pets. Kat Albrecht

Dog Friendly Gardens, Garden Friendly Dogs. Cheryl Smith

Dog Language, An Encyclopedia of Canine Behavior. Roger Abrantes

Evolution of Canine Social Behavior, 2nd ed. Roger Abrantes

Fighting Dominance in a Dog Whispering World, DVD. Jean Donaldson and Ian Dunbar

Focus Not Fear. Training Insights from a Reactive Dog Class. Ali Brown

Give Them a Scalpel and They Will Dissect a Kiss, DVD. Ian Dunbar

Guide To Professional Dog Walking And Home Boarding. Dianne Eibner

How To Run A Dog Business: Putting Your Career Where Your Heart Is. Veronica Boutelle

Language of Dogs, DVD. Sarah Kalnajs

Mastering Variable Surface Tracking, Component Tracking (2 bk set). Ed Presnall

Mindful Dog Teaching: Reflections on the Relationships We Share with our Dogs. Claudeen McAuliffe

My Dog Pulls. What Do I Do? Turid Rugaas

New Knowledge of Dog Behavior (reprint). Clarence Pfaffenberger

On Talking Terms with Dogs: Calming Signals, 2nd edition. Turid Rugaas

On Talking Terms with Dogs: What Your Dog Tells You, DVD. Turid Rugaas

Positive Perspectives: Love Your Dog, Train Your Dog. Pat Miller

Positive Perspectives 2: Know Your Dog, Train Your Dog. Pat Miller

Positive Training for Show Dogs: Building a Relationship for Success. Vicki Ronchette

Predation and Family Dogs, DVD. Jean Donaldson

Really Reliable Recall.
Train Your Dog to Come When Called, DVD. Leslie Nelson
Right on Target.
Taking Dog Training to a New Level. Mandy Book & Cheryl Smith
Stress in Dogs. Martina Scholz & Clarissa von Reinhardt
The Dog Trainer's Resource: The APDT Chronicle of the Dog Collection.
Mychelle Blake (*ed*)
Therapy Dogs: Training Your Dog To Reach Others.
Kathy Diamond Davis
Training Dogs, A Manual (reprint). Konrad Most
Training the Disaster Search Dog. Shirley Hammond
Try Tracking: The Puppy Tracking Primer. Carolyn Krause
Visiting the Dog Park, Having Fun, and Staying Safe. Cheryl S. Smith
When Pigs Fly. Train Your Impossible Dog. Jane Killion
Winning Team. A Guidebook for Junior Showmanship. Gail Haynes
Working Dogs (reprint). Elliot Humphrey & Lucien Warner

HEALTH & ANATOMY, SHOWING
An Eye for a Dog. Illustrated Guide to Judging Purebred Dogs. Robert Cole
Annie On Dogs! Ann Rogers Clark
Canine Cineradiography, DVD. Rachel Page Elliott
Canine Massage: A Complete Reference Manual.
Jean-Pierre Hourdebaigt
Canine Terminology (reprint). Harold Spira
Dog In Action (reprint). Macdowell Lyon
Dogsteps DVD. Rachel Page Elliott
Performance Dog Nutrition: Optimize Performance With Nutrition.
Jocelynn Jacobs
Puppy Intensive Care: A Breeder's Guide To Care Of Newborn Puppies.
Myra Savant Harris
Raw Dog Food: Make It Easy for You and Your Dog. Carina MacDonald
Raw Meaty Bones. Tom Lonsdale
Shock to the System. The Facts About Animal Vaccination...
Catherine O'Driscoll
The History and Management of the Mastiff. Elizabeth Baxter & Pat Hoffman
Work Wonders. Feed Your Dog Raw Meaty Bones. Tom Lonsdale
Whelping Healthy Puppies, DVD. Sylvia Smart

Dogwise.com is your complete source for dog books on the web!

2,000+ titles, fast shipping, and excellent customer service.